Wisdom of the East

PRECIOUS JEWELS OF GREAT WISDOM
GARNERED FROM THE SAGES
OF INDIA AND THE
FAR ORIENT

Compiled by Elisabeth Deane

GIFTS OF GOLD
———
THE PETER PAUPER PRESS, INC.
MOUNT VERNON, NEW YORK

SEVEN thou shalt not neglect: thy wife as long as she lives in peace with thee, thy livelihood as long as it provides for thee, thy ornament as long as it adorns thee, thy friend as long as he is just to thee, thy table companion as long as he understands thee, thy son as long as he cannot take care of himself, and thy guest as long as he does not molest thee.

Wisdom of the East

HONOR thy father, and thy son will honor thee.

WHEN a consuming desire to steal another's goods is transformed into action, the result is endless woe.

IF you keep looking for faults, at last even your relatives will leave you.

A LEARNED man who gives good advice to others and forgets of himself is to be compared with the wick of a lamp which spends light to others, while its own self wastes away.

THREE are not to be trusted: the steadiness of a horse, the favor of a king and the faith of women.

THE prudent takes no poison even if he possesses the antidote.

Do not act too familiarly with the noble, for he will feel offended; nor with the vile, for he will become insolent toward thee.

6

A FOOL gives a nut to him who has no teeth. He gives advice to one who has not the means to follow it.

NOT he who can extricate himself from difficulties is the prudent one, but he who cautiously bewares not to intricate himself.

IT IS better that thou shouldst guard thy secret than that another one should guard it.

HE who proves things by experience increases his knowledge; he who believes blindly increases his errors.

THE following are good when joined together: Learning joined with the fear of God, memory with genius, beauty with kindness, nobility of descent with good morals, joy with security, riches with contentment, and endeavor with the help of God.

A SMILING enemy is like a colocynth, it has green leaves, but its taste kills.

MEN eat greedily; more greedily, however, time eats them.

Two are not to be satiated: he that seeks knowledge and he that seeks riches.

8

To refuse in a kind manner is better than to make promises which are not kept.

Beware of thy enemy once, of thy friends a thousand times.

Thy secret is thy prisoner if thou keepest it; thou art its prisoner if thou divulgest it.

A wound inflicted by speech is more painful than a wound inflicted by the sword.

Bad morals destroy what the ancestors have built.

9

ELOQUENCE consists in making the speech comprehensible to the multitude and agreeable to the learned.

WATER is the most indifferent thing as long as we have it, — the most precious as soon as we want it.

ON entering every one feels embarrassed; the remedy is a friendly greeting.

ENVY is like rust on iron, that leaves it not until it corrodes it.

To be inclined to anger is in the nature of boys; to mourn the past is in the nature of women.

IF traveling in the land of the one-eyed, put out one of thy eyes.

≈

MANKIND consists of two men; one who takes heed, the other of whom heed is taken.

≈

Do not confine your children to your own learning, for they were born in another time.

≈

WHEN the son's beard begins to grow shave thy own beard.

≈

BE submissive in thy childhood that thou mayest be respected in thy old age.

II

IF you can solve the knot with the tongue, do not solve it with the teeth.

∾

HE who excuses himself without having given offense makes himself suspected of it.

∾

Do not trust him who lies for thee, for he is as ready to lie against thee.

∾

WHO asks more of a friend than he can bestow deserves to be refused.

∾

EVERY bird rejoices in its own voice.

THREE make lean — a slow messenger, a lamp that does not shine, and the expectation to dine at the table of him who is yet to come.

BEWARE of too much laughter, for it deadens the mind and produces oblivion.

THE beginning of anger is madness; the end is penitence.

A MAN cannot be blamed for not being of noble origin.

OLD age is sickness enough.

THY right hand shall not inflict injury upon thy left hand. (Be just to thy own kind.)

TREAT thy subordinate with kindness, thy equal with justice and thy superior with prudence.

Do unto thy brother as thou wouldst have him do unto thee.

A FRIENDLY smile is a key to security and a lamp to benevolence.

INSTRUCTION in the time of youth is like the sculpture on a stone.

A FACE without bashfulness is like a log whose bark has been peeled off, and like a lamp whose oil has been consumed.

❧

HE who fatigues his body brings peace to his mind.

❧

NOTHING that comes from heaven is more bitter than the cup of blindness.

❧

SPEECH is a beautiful net in which souls are caught.

❧

THE enemy of thy father, as long as he lives, will never be thy friend.

For three things there is no remedy: Poverty associated with laziness, sickness coupled with old age, and enmity mixed with envy.

Weakness married laziness and their progeny was poverty.

None will scratch my back but my own nail, and none will hasten my business but my own foot.

The egg of today is better than the hen of tomorrow.

He who accepts the promise of security from an enemy is not free from danger.

THE heart of the fool is in his tongue; the tongue of the prudent is in his heart.

❧

WHY is the flap of the ear soft? That one may press it into the cavity of the ear when he hears objectionable words.

❧

THE friend of a king is like one that rides on a lion: men fear him, and he fears the animal on which he rides.

❧

HE who administers to a king should enter blind and leave mute.

❧

A LITTLE bread is better than a thousand words.

Not every one who is covered with a leopard skin is a hero.

When the hawk grows old the sparrows mock him.

Two are to be pitied: the noble in the power of the vile, and the wise in the power of the fool.

Every moment of time carries away a part of thy life.

Thy morning time is a fox, thy evening a wolf. In youth we are beguiled by time; in old age we are devoured by it.

BE not of those who publicly curse the devil, and secretly serve him.

❧

BEAUTY is the wisdom of women, and wisdom is the beauty of men.

❧

THE avaricious is the guardian of his riches and the treasurer of his heir.

❧

KNOWLEDGE is like a mountain: difficult to ascend but easy to descend.

❧

HE who buys bread with borrowed money, have compassion on him; he who buys meat with borrowed money, throw at him a stone.

19

WHEN thy neighbor shaves his beard, soap thou thine.

❧

NOT every one who searches finds, and not every one who flees escapes.

❧

RICHES and all worldly things perish; good deeds remain.

❧

WHEN the rich man tells a lie all say, "It is true;" and when he dances all say, "How beautiful it is!"

❧

THE fox favored by fortune conquers the lion favored by strength.

RICHES are like water in the house, whose channels are obstructed; if it finds no exit it drowns the owner.

❧

IF thou hast not what thou desirest, desire what thou hast.

❧

THE greatest delight for the inhabitants of Paradise is the consciousness that it will not end.

❧

HEALTH is better than medicine; not to sin is better than to be forgiven.

❧

How many poor are rich in mind, and how many rich are poor in mind.

To abstain from the prohibited is better than to seek after the permitted.

THE best of men is he who sees his own faults and does not see the faults of others.

THE remedy for him who has no remedy is patience.

HE is the wise man whose action, word, and thought are one and the same.

RICHES and all worldly things perish; good deeds remain.

THE wise realize that some day they will have gray hair. Therefore, while young, they refuse to be slaves to the world. But those who try to remain young cannot overcome their faults. They have not stability. At the end of their lives you will see them painfully trying with their canes to get upon their feet.

~✿

TRUE pleasure comes from moral living. All other pleasures are linked with trouble and win no praise.

~✿

ONLY the wise have real eyes. But the foolish man has two sores in the sockets where his eyes should be.

23

THE days fly past. Suddenly Death comes as though in anger. Therefore let man realize that wealth too will pass away, and let him begin now to lead a life of virtue.

WISE men know that the body is the seat of disease and sin. So let a man learn to live without enslavement to the body and in detachment from it, like drops of water on a lily leaf. Such men do not talk about this with others.

As the lovely swan seeks within a lake the beautiful lotus, so noble men will seek their own kind. As the crow flies hungrily to the corpse of the funeral pyre, so ignoble men will seek their own level.

ONCE there was a Brahmin whose enemy was a hunter. One day the hunter saved the Brahmin's life. Likewise there was a king who had a pet monkey. The monkey, not knowing what it did, killed the king. These incidents prove that a wise man, though considered an enemy, may become a true friend; while an ignoramus, considered a friend, is a potential enemy.

As the poor man stands humbly in the presence of the wealthy, so the noble will seek knowledge from men of learning. They who crave not knowledge will remain ignoble.

THE mother and the father are the first gods that children know.

THERE are those people who prefer eating to listening to the wise. What does it matter if such ignorant beings should live or die?

❧

MAKE friends of those whose friendship is like that of the dog, rather than that of the elephant. Even though an elephant has known its master for a long time, it may one day kill him. But a dog, even when his master has thrust a spear through its body, will still affectionately wag its tail.

❧

'TIS good to see good people; to listen to their words, and speak of their good qualities is also good. But best of all is it to live with them in close association.

Some folks are like the betel tree: their friendship must be cultivated daily or it will fail. Others are the friends who resemble the cocoanut tree, needing constant care in the early stages only. Best of all are the friends who, like the palmyra tree, planted on a sandy plain, after the first day bears fruit, and needs no further care.

When starvation comes, honor, high birth, learning, knowledge, almsgiving, the performance of austerities, high rank, industry, and the desire for women — all these will vanish.

As the water of a well increases in proportion to the amount drawn, so learning increases with the effort put forth.

As the husk, separated from the paddy, loses some of its strength, so when two friends long separated become reunited, something of the firmness of their former relationship is lost.

SINCE life is but a bubble, wealth like wind-driven waves, and the body like letters written in water, why not turn to God?

Is anything more cruel or hateful than the anger which destroys the smile upon the face and the love within the heart? If one would really guard himself, let him beware of anger, or it will destroy him! The fire of anger, which burns up all that comes near, will also burn up the pleasant raft of friendship.

IF rainfall is scanty, none can increase it. If rain is abundant, none can decrease it. Likewise none can avert the joys and the sorrows he is destined to receive.

WOMAN, even though you dip a two-quart pail into the ocean, it will not hold eight quarts! In the same way, the securing of a husband and much property depends on how you behaved in a previous life.

GREATEST of all forms of wealth is the wealth of kindness. Material goods are riches to fools only. They who seek the virtue of kindness must practice it. It will be found that kindness should be shown to all life upon the earth. So it is that one should eat only after giving alms.

29

O YOU stupid man! Do you imagine that you, instead of God, control events? Those who look for fruit on the magnolia tree may find only poison. All events are the outcome of the deeds in a previous life.

EVEN though what's eaten be the food of immortality, it is unfitting to eat alone while guests are waiting outside the home.

LET what you speak behind another's back be the same as what you say in his presence.

THE essence of virtue is to refrain from taking life; murder is conducive to all other sins.

As there are trees which bear fruit but do not blossom, so there are men who act without having to be directed. Talking to a fool is like sowing seed which does not germinate. Even though you take great pains to explain things to a fool, he will not understand.

REVENGE upon a wrong-doer brings only one day's pleasure. For him who bears with patience evil from another, there will be praise until the world shall end.

A MAN will not say, "My father became poor because he gave to beggars, so I'll not give to them!" Rather is he like the sapling underneath the banana tree, continuing to bear fruit after its parent dies.

IF one becomes angry with another who is stronger than he, he harms himself only. And though his anger should temporarily succeed, the result will be sin and evil. There is nothing more harmful than anger.

DESPISE not patient folk who may appear ignorant. Note the patient, motionless stork which stands on the bank of a pond, waiting for its prey, the fish, to swim near.

SWEET it is to enjoy one's food in the presence of God, one's ancestors, relatives and guests. They who know no such enjoyment are like the stork, which gobbles down in solitude the fish which it has caught.

LET him who knows not books listen to those who do. Such learning is a staff on which to lean in trouble.

~

As the sun shrivels the spineless worm, so God will punish the man who has no love.

~

To refrain from killing and eating the flesh of what is killed is the highest type of the ascetic life.

~

JUST as a calf will easily find its mother in a herd of cows, so the deeds of one's life will hunt him out in his next life. In other words, the deeds done by a man in this life will have an unfailing effect upon his next one.

33

THE venomous cobra lives in hiding, but the harmless watersnake wriggles about fearlessly in the open. So the deceitful in mind will hide themselves; while the guileless man will move about freely.

SEEK no food for your stomach while you have the opportunity to learn by listening.

THE great are they who attempt the different things, which lesser men avoid.

IF the housewife be of good character, what can the home lack? If she be not such, of what use the home?

34

THE learned say that the wife's chastity is the good fortune of the home, and that good children are the home's decoration.

AMONG all who walk in a depraved way, there is no greater fool than the man who stands in the doorway of the house of another, lusting for his wife.

THE false embrace of money-loving courtesans is like to that of pallbearers, who for money embrace a corpse in a dark room.

SWEETER than ambrosia are the hands of little children held up for food.

MEN unfit for friendship are like the water fowl, which abandons a pond after the water is gone. Real friends are like the water lily; they remain to share both prosperity and adversity.

HE who entertains the guests who come to him, and all who follow after, will be a welcome guest in heaven.

ARGUE not with a fool! If you talk with him, he will twist your words in reply. 'Tis best if possible to slip away from him.

To behave with impartiality toward neighbor, friend and foe, is the height of virtue.

WISDOM, benevolence, and fortitude — these three are the universal virtues. The means by which they are practiced is another thing. Some are born with a knowledge of these duties; some know them by study; some gain them as the result of painful experience. But the knowledge being possessed, it comes to one and the same thing. Some practice them with the ease of nature; some for the sake of their advantage; and some by dint of great effort. But when the work of them is done, it comes to one and the same thing.

ORPHANS, an old man without sons, an old man who has lost his wife, and an old woman who has lost her husband; these four were considered as the most forlorn of heaven's people, for they had none to whom they could tell their wants.

HAVING not, yet affecting to have; empty, yet affecting to be full; straitened, yet affecting to be in easy circumstances, — it is difficult with such characteristics to be consistent. Ardent, yet not upright; stupid, and yet not attentive; simple, and yet not sincere, — such persons I do not understand.

I HAVE not seen one who loves virtue as he loves beauty. The doings of the Supreme Heaven have neither sound nor smell. That is perfect virtue.

RESPECT shown without observing the rules of propriety is called vulgarity. Courtesy without observing these rules, is called forwardness. Boldness without observing them is called violence. Forwardness mars gentleness and benevolence.

HUMANITY is like a heavy vessel, and like a long road. He who tries to lift the vessel cannot sustain its weight; he who travels the road cannot accomplish all its distance. There is nothing that has so many different degrees as humanity; and thus who tries to nerve himself to compass it finds it a difficult task.

To LIE under arms and meet death without regret — this is the strength of Northern regions, and the strong make it their study. To show forbearance and gentleness in teaching others, and not revenge unreasonable conduct, this is the strength of Southern regions, and the good man makes it his study.

A MINISTER, in serving his prince, reverently discharges his duties, and makes his emolument a

secondary consideration. Truly straightforward was the historiographer Yu. When good government prevailed in his State, he was like an arrow. When bad government prevailed, he was like an arrow.

HE WHO aims to be a man of complete virtue, does not seek in his food to gratify his appetite, nor in his dwelling-place does he seek his ease; he is in earnest in what he is doing, and careful in his speech; he frequents the company of men of principle that he may be kept upright. Such a person may be said indeed to love to learn.

FROM the Emperor down to the masses of the people, all must consider the cultivation of the person the root of everything else.

To see men of worth and not be able to raise them to office; to raise them to office and not be able to do so quickly, — this is treating them with disrespect. To see bad men and not be able to remove them; to remove them, but not to send them far away, — this is weakness. If good men were to govern a country a hundred years, they would be able to transform the violently bad, and dispense with capital punishments.

The rules of propriety are simply the principle of reverence. Therefore the reverence paid to a father makes the sons pleased. The reverence paid to an elder brother makes younger brothers pleased. The reverence paid to a ruler makes subjects pleased. The reverence paid to one man makes myriads pleased. The reverence is paid to a few, and the pleasure extends to the many.

THE scholar recommends members of his own family to public employment without hesitation because of their kinship, and proposes others without regard to their enmity to him. He estimates men's merits, and takes into consideration all their services, selecting those of virtue and ability, putting them forward without expecting any recompense from them. The ruler thus gets what he wishes, and if benefit results to the State, the scholar does not seek riches or honors for himself. Such is his place in promotion and employment of the worthy and bringing forward the able.

THE rules aimed at in the Great College were the prevention of evil before it was manifested; the timeliness of instruction just when it was required; the suitability of the lessons in adaptation to circumstances; and the good influence of ex-

ample to all those concerned. It was from these four things that the teaching was so flourishing.

THE master who skillfully waits to be questioned may be compared to a bell when it is struck. Struck with a small hammer, it gives a small sound; struck with a great one, it gives a great sound. But let it be struck leisurely and properly, and it gives out all the sound of which it is capable.

CEREMONIAL feasting accompanied by drinking was not intended to have bad effects; yet cases of litigation were more numerous in consequence of it. It is the excessive drinking which produces the evil. Therefore the old kings framed rules to regulate drinking. Where there is but one pres-

43

entation of the cup at one time, guest and host may bow to each other a hundred times without getting drunk. This was the way in which those kings guarded against this evil.

❧

WHAT you do not like when done to yourself, do not do to others.

❧

TO BE fond of learning is near to wisdom; to practice with vigor is near to benevolence; and to be conscious of shame is near to fortitude. He who knows these three things knows how to cultivate his own character. Knowing how to cultivate his own character, he knows how to govern other men. Knowing how to govern other men, he knows how to govern the kingdom, with its States and families.

44

Hung Tzu-ch'eng of the Ming Dynasty

Most people can read a book with words but not one without words, and they can play a lyre with strings but not one without strings. How can they derive tranquil pleasure from a book or a lyre, when they exercise their intelligence only on the material, but not on the spiritual, aspect of things?

The larger the fortune hoarded, the greater the loss. The higher the climb, the quicker the fall.

When a man, with a jar of wine beside him, takes the heavens as a tent and the earth as a mat, he is in harmony with the life-giving forces. Who can say that inebriety is not a way to practice Ch'anist meditation?

45

ACTORS paint their faces with powder and rouge in order to imitate Beauty or Ugliness. Where is their beauty or ugliness, after their songs are finished and the audience gone away? Chessplayers contend avidly with each other in their moves in order to determine who will be the victor and who the vanquished. Where is their victory or defeat, after the game is over and the pieces are wrapped up?

THOSE who express loathing for pomp and vainglory might, on encountering them, revel in them. Those who profess rejoicing at contentment and simplicity might, in experiencing them, become bored with them. So one must sweep away enthusiasm and indifference, eliminate predilection and aversion, forget pomp and vainglory, and delight in contentment and simplicity.

46

WHEN the wind blows through the scattered bamboos, they do not hold its sound after it has gone. When the wild geese fly over a cold lake, it does not retain their shadows after they have passed. So the mind of the superior man begins to work only when an event occurs; and it becomes a void again when the matter ends.

HUMAN affairs are like a chess-game: only those who do not take it seriously can be called good players. Life is like an earthen pot: only when it is shattered, does it manifest its emptiness.

THE SPIRIT of man communes with Heaven; the omnipotence of Heaven resides in man. Is the distance between Heaven and man very great?

To CONCUR with a web of circumstances is to dismiss it, and is like the harmony between flitting butterflies and fluttering flowers. To accord with an event is to nullify it, and is like the perfection of the full moon as round as a basin of water.

To BOAST of fame is not such a pleasure as to avoid it; to be versed in worldly affairs does not bring such leisure as to be unconcerned with them. Lo, a lone cloud idling across a mountain peak does not care whether it stays there or passes on; while the bright moon hanging in the firmament is indifferent as to whether the world is silent or noisy.

STRAYING from Enlightenment, a man finds a happy land to be a sea of suffering, as water is

frozen into ice; but awakening to Enlightenment, he discovers a sea of suffering to be a happy land, as ice is melted into water. Hence, we know that suffering and happiness are not two different moods and that straying from, and awakening to, Enlightenment are not two different frames of mind.

A DROP of water has the tastes of the water of the seven seas: there is no need to experience all the ways of worldly life. The reflections of the moon on one thousand rivers are from the same moon: the mind must be full of light.

MANURE-WORMS are dirty, and yet they transform themselves into cicadas, which drink dew in the autumnal wind. Decayed grasses are not bright,

49

and yet they give birth to glow-worms, whose luster matches the summer moon. Hence we know that cleanliness often comes from filth and brilliance from gloom.

WHEN the mind is possessed of reality, it feels tranquil and joyous even without music or song, and it produces a pure fragrance even without incense or tea.

As THERE is the clear sky with the bright moon, whither can moths not fly? But they dash only into night candles. As there are clear fountains and green bamboos, what can barn-owls not drink and peck? But they are fond of putrid rats. Alas, are not many people in the world like moths and barn-owls?

Looking at the busy bees in a fragrant and luxuriant garden, one may become disillusioned about the life of the senses and the ways of the world. Beholding the sleeping swallows in a quiet and humble hovel, one may arouse in oneself a cool pleasure and a deep contemplation.

When a man's mind is as limpid as if it were a burnished mirror or a still pond, there is under the heavens nothing detestable. And when his temper is as serene as if he were under the beautiful sun and in the light breezes, there is on the earth no one hideous.

Whether in favor or in humiliation, be not dismayed. Let your eyes leisurely look at the flowers

blooming and falling in your courtyard. Whether you leave or retain your position, take no care. Let your mind wander with the clouds folding and unfolding beyond the horizon.

WHETHER time is long or short, and whether space is broad or narrow, depend upon the mind. Those whose minds are at leisure can feel one day as long as a millennium, and those whose thought is expansive can perceive a small house to be as spacious as the universe.

THOSE who prefer quietude to noise retreat from people into solitude, but they do not know that to be alone is a self-obsession and to aim at quiescence is the root of action.

By the side of honor, humiliation waits. When honored, one ought not be high-spirited. Behind poverty, prosperity follows. When impoverished, why should one be low-spirited?

If a man could clear the meanness from his face, his looks would show no ugliness. And if he could empty the worldliness from his heart, his language would bear high meanings.

While a crane is standing among chickens, it may be said to be incomparably pre-ëminent. But if it looks at a roc flying over the wide sea, it finds itself dwarfed. Moreover, if it gazes at a phoenix soaring towards the zenith, it feels itself infinitely smaller.

Fɪsʜɪɴɢ is a pleasure of retirement, yet the angler has the power to let the fish live or die. Chess-playing is an enjoyable pastime, yet the players are motivated by the idea of war.

Eᴠᴇɴ if a man has clenched the past and the present in his two fists, he has finally to release them. And if he has shouldered the wind and the moon with a bamboo-cane, he has eventually to unload them.

Wʜᴇɴ there is no commotion and agitation in a man's mind, he finds every place as peaceful as a verdant hill or a green tree. When there are transforming and nurturing powers in his nature, he discovers every thing as lively as a leaping fish or a flying hawk.

A REAL man is one whose goodness is a part of himself. Of all the qualities of the sage, none is greater than that of being a helper of men to right living. He is ashamed of a reputation beyond his desert. Having found the right way within himself, he rests in it, firm and serene, holding intimate converse with it, and reaching to its fountain-head. He obeys the right and waits for the appointed. His words are plain and simple, yet of widest bearing. His aim is self-culture, yet it gives peace to all men.

LET not a man do what his sense of right bids him not to do, nor desire what it forbids him to desire. This is sufficient. The skillful artist will not alter his measures for the sake of a stupid workman.

55

THE honor which man confers is not true honor. Those to whom Chaou Mang gave rank, he can degrade again. He whose good name comes from what he is, needs no trappings. The ancients cultivated the nobility of Heaven, leaving that of men to follow in its train. Serving Heaven consists in nourishing the real constitution of our being, anxious neither about death nor life.

THE virtues are not poured into us, they are natural: seek, and you will find them; neglect and you will lose them. To every faculty and relation belongs its normal law; but without fit culture it will decay. How lamentable to lose this virtue and not know how to seek it! The virtue of all seeds is in their ripeness. Only he who has studied his mental constitution knows his nature; knowing his nature, he knows Heaven.

56

ALL things are already complete in us. There is no greater delight than to be conscious of right within us. If one strives to treat others as he would be treated by them, he shall not fail to come near the perfect life.

Every duty is a charge, but the charge of oneself is the root of all others.

The disease of men is to neglect their own fields and go to weeding those of others, to exact much from others and lay light burdens on themselves. A true scholar holds possession of himself, neither by riches nor poverty forced away from his virtue.

THE great man is he who does not lose his child-heart. He does not think beforehand that his words shall be sincere, nor that his acts shall be resolute; he simply abides in the right.

When Heaven is about to confer a great office on any man, it first disciplines his mind with suffering, and his bones and sinews with toil. It exposes him to want and subjects him to extreme poverty. It confounds his undertakings. By all these methods it stimulates his mind, hardens him, and supplies his incompetencies.

When men die of famine, you say it is the season that is to blame. What does this differ from saying, when you have caused a man's death, "It was not I, but the weapon?"

Life springs from calamity, and death from ease. Men of special virtue and wisdom are wont to owe these powers to the trials they have endured.

THERE is something, chaotic yet complete, which existed before Heaven and Earth. Oh, how still it is and formless, standing alone without changing, reaching everywhere without suffering harm! It must be regarded as the Mother of the Universe. Its name I know not. To designate it I call it Tao. Endeavoring to describe it, I call it great.

HE WHO knows others is clever, but he who knows himself is enlightened. He who overcomes others is strong, but he who overcomes himself is mightier still. He is rich who knows when he has enough. He who acts with energy has strength of purpose. He who moves not from his proper place is long-lasting. He who dies, but perishes not, enjoys true longevity.

59

THE TAO that can be trodden is not the enduring and unchanging Tao. He who knows the Tao does not care to speak about it; he who is ever ready to speak about it does not know it. Those who know the Tao are not extensively learned; the extensively learned do not know it.

THE skillful philosophers of the olden times were subtle, spiritual, profound, and penetrating. They were so deep as to be incomprehensible. Because they are hard to comprehend, I will endeavor to describe them. Shrinking were they, like one fording a stream in winter. Cautious were they, like one who fears an attack from any quarter. Circumspect were they, like a stranger guest; self-effacing, like ice about to melt; simple, like un-polished wood; vacant, like a valley; opaque, like muddy water.

WHEN the superior scholar hears of Tao, he diligently practices it. When the average scholar hears of Tao, he sometimes retains it, sometimes loses it. When the inferior scholar hears of Tao, he loudly laughs at it. Were it not thus ridiculed, it would not be worthy of the name of Tao.

THE TAO which can be expressed in words is not the eternal Tao; the name which can be uttered is not its eternal name. Without a name, it is the beginning of Heaven and Earth; with a name, it is the Mother of all things.

HE WHO respects the State as his own person is fit to govern it. He who loves the State as his own body is fit to be intrusted with it.

ALL things alike do their work, and then we see them subside. When they have reached their bloom, each returns to its origin. Returning to their origin means rest or fulfillment of destiny. This reversion is an eternal law. To know that law is to be enlightened. Not to know it, is misery and calamity. He who knows the eternal law is liberal-minded. Being liberal-minded, he is just. Being just, he is kingly. Being kingly, he is akin to Heaven. Being akin to Heaven, he possesses Tao. Possessed of Tao, he endures forever. Though his body perish, yet he suffers no harm.

THESE two things, the spiritual and the material, though we call them by different names, in their origin are one and the same. This sameness is a mystery, — the mystery of mysteries. It is the gate of all spirituality.